A Little Book About SAFETY

ISBN 978-0-545-86294-3

Published by Scholastic Inc., 557 Broadway, New York, NY 10012,
by arrangement with The Mother Company/Ruby's Studio.

12 11 10 9 8 7 6 5 4 3 16 17 18 19 20/0

Printed in the U.S.A. 40

First Scholastic printing, April 2015

Book Design: Rae Friis

from the award-winning

RUBY'S STUDIO: THE SAFETY SHOW

A Little Book About SAFETY

Written by: Samantha Kurtzman-Counter & Abbie Schiller
Based on a screenplay by: Ruby Vanderzee
Illustration: François Grumelin-Sohn, Laura Sicouri, Martin Carolo

SCHOLASTIC INC.

THE MOTHER COMPANY

Meet my friend, Hugo.
He is 6 years old. Today, he's going swimming with his family. Let's count all the ways Hugo keeps himself safe.

Hugo loves the warm sand and the salty sea air – he's so excited and can't wait to dive into the water!

The Hippo family meets a friendly goose at the entrance. "Welcome to the Happy Herd Community Pool," she says. "Name and phone number, please."

Hugo tries to answer.
"My name is Hugo Hippo,
and my phone
number is… 508… 555…"

All the numbers start mixing up in his head.
Hugo can't remember his phone number!

Mama Hippo is there to help. "It's 508-555-0873."
She gives Hugo a big hug.
"Maybe we just need to keep practicing it."

Hugo goes into the changing room,
and puts on his favorite blue swim trunks.
He's ready to swim!

"I'm heading over to the diving board, Dad," Hugo says.
"OK, I'll watch you from here," Daddy Hippo replies.

Hugo decides today he's going on the super-sky-high diving board. He climbs the stairs all the way to the tippy-top.

But once Hugo gets to the top, he feels scared.
He gets shaky and his tummy feels tingly.
"Uh-oh. NO WAY. Too high," he thinks and
decides to climb back down.

As Hugo goes down the stairs, he isn't scared anymore. He stops shaking and his tummy feels fine.

"Smart choice, dude," the toad says to Hugo. "You can try again when you're bigger," adds the cricket by his side. "Yeah," Hugo replies. He knows he made a safe decision.

As Hugo gets ready to jump off the lower diving board, two sneaky monkeys swing down and tickle him!

"Stop that!" Hugo says. "Keep your hands to yourselves, silly monkeys." The monkeys say "sorry" and leave Hugo alone.

Hugo takes a running start, bounces on the board and flies into the water with a big SPLASH!

After a short swim, Hugo sees an ostrich next to the pool selling ice cream. "Slugpops! Bugsicles! Frog Tongue Slurpees!" calls the ostrich.

"Could you do me a favor and go get me more Bugsicles from my truck?" the ostrich says to Hugo. "I'll give you a free Slugpop if you do. It'll be our little secret."

Hugo thinks about what the ostrich asked him to do. Even though Hugo loves Slugpops, is it safe to go to the parking lot by himself?

"No!" says Hugo.
"I have to go check with my parents first."

SAFETY TIP
— NO. 7 —
Thumbs up, Hugo!
If anyone - even someone you already know - asks you to go anywhere or do anything unexpected, check with a Safe Adult first.
CREAM

Hugo tries to find his family, but he doesn't see them anywhere! He feels scared. Where are they?

SAFETY TIP
— NO. 8 —

If you ever get lost, just stop right where you are and yell for your Safe Adult.

Hugo sees a little mouse mama having lunch with her tiny mouse babies. Maybe she can help Hugo find his family! "Excuse me, ma'am," he asks, "Can you help me find my parents?"

"Why, of course sonny!"
The mama mouse replies, taking out her tiny phone. "Do you know their phone number?"

Hugo freezes. Can he do it? Will he remember?

Hugo concentrates really hard. "508...555..." This is the part he always forgets - but not this time! "0-8-7-3!" Hugo smiles from ear to ear. He finally remembered Mama Hippo's phone number!

"Hello?" Mama answers. Hugo turns his head and sees that she is right behind him. "Mama!" he says and runs into her arms.

Mama hugs her little hippo tightly. "I'm so proud of you," she says. Hugo hugs her back. "I love you, Mama," he replies.

Hugo spends the rest of the day playing by the water with his family, confident that all his smart choices will help keep him strong, happy and SAFE.

a note to
PARENTS & TEACHERS

Nothing is more important than keeping our children safe — but how can we talk to our kids about personal safety without scaring them? How can we be sure they know what to do to keep themselves safe when we're not around?

In **A Little Book About Safety**, we offer a modern, empowering approach to kids' personal safety. We address potentially lifesaving issues with no scare tactics and no "ick factor." Working closely with child safety expert Pattie Fitzgerald of Safely Ever After, Inc., we came up with a relatable story that kids will love to read while absorbing essential safety tools and tips they can use in their everyday lives.

When lovable Hugo Hippo navigates his way through a fun day at the community pool with his family, his safety readiness is put to the test in a variety of familiar situations. He realizes he needs to memorize his safe adult's phone number in case he gets lost, he remembers to cover up his private parts when changing to swim, he trusts his own internal "Uh-Oh Feeling" inside when deciding not to jump off the super-high diving board, and he remembers to "Check First" with a safe adult before going anywhere unexpected. These and other important safety lessons are explored gently and with humor, offering clear, safe solutions to decisions about safety that kids have to make every day.

At The Mother Company, our aim is to help parents and educators in the job of raising healthy, happy, and self-reliant children. We believe that children ought to be armed with all the information they need to make safe and smart decisions. Knowledge is power and with our Safety Series of videos, books, apps, and activity kits, we are dedicated to empowering children to be smart about safety.

For more resources to help keep kids safe, visit us at TheMotherCo.com.

– Abbie Schiller and Sam Kurtzman-Counter, The Mother Company Mamas

m THE MOTHER COMPANY
HELPING PARENTS RAISE GOOD PEOPLE WITH FUN, AWARD-WINNING BOOKS & VIDEOS
The Feelings Series
FEELINGS SHOW
A Little Book About FEELINGS
WHEN MILES GOT MAD
Sally Simon Simmons' Super Frustrating Day
"Edutainment at its best!" - Daily Candy
The Safety Series
SAFETY SHOW
A Little Book About SAFETY
MILES IS THE BOSS OF HIS BODY
When Lyla Got Lost (and found)
The Friendship Series
FRIENDSHIP SHOW
A LITTLE BOOK ABOUT FRIENDSHIP
ONE FOR ALL
Casey Caterpillar feels left out
★★★★★ 5 stars! - Common Sense Media
SEE WHAT'S NEW AT THEMOTHERCO.COM
INTRODUCING OUR SIBLINGS SERIES!
SIBLINGS SHOW
WINNER
Cynopsis Kids Imagination AWARDS
2012 PRODUCT of the Year Award
SMART BOOK
2013 NATIONAL Parenting Publications AWARDS HONORS
DR TOY'S 2013
KIDS FIRST!
The National Parenting Center Seal of Approval
2012 DVD of the Year Award